The Dreams We Share

Poems by

Raphael Block

Cover design by Judyth Greenburgh
Cover art by Gerald Macua, geraldmacuaphoto.com

Books by Raphael Block:

Songs from a Small Universe
Spangling Darkness
Strings of Shining Silence
At This Table

Spangling Darkness and Strings of Shining Silence are
available as free audio downloads at raphaelblock.com

ISBN: 978-1-63649-694-8

Poetic Matrix Press
www.poeticmatrix.com

Dedication

To our Mother, for each breath She gives.

Contents

Ablaze

New Home

The Heaven I Carry

We, the Healers

In Gratitude

About the Author

Preface

We can create a new civilization with our dreams, thoughts, feelings, and actions—and many of us are already doing so. Our current civilization is beyond saving because it is totally unsustainable.

Gaia needs us to listen, to learn from our elders who lived, and even flourished, for billions or hundreds of millions of years through her ever-changing ways and ages. The rocks, trees, insects, and the millions of species that call Earth home have wisdom of tremendous value to share with us if we are open to experiencing and witnessing them. Professor Robin Wall Kimmerer, a member of the Citizen Potawatomi Nation, describes, for example, lessons that we could draw from the many different mosses.[1]

Once we consider the elements that make up our world, know them for the great beings they are—beginning with water, the basis of all life—we can align ourselves with natural laws, or core principles. These natural laws affirm the necessity for giving and receiving, and the value of meeting each being's unique needs.

Utopian! one might exclaim. Yet every day it becomes clearer that our very survival depends on our alignment with these fundamental laws. The Covid pandemic has revealed our utter dependency on each other, has shown us what is essential and non-essential work, as well as the fragility of our institutions based on man-made laws that have little relationship to the miraculous beings that shape every moment of our days, starting, yes, with the molecules we breathe, expressed as a breeze of flowing waves through branches, bushes, grasses, birdsong, and the dreams we share.

Footstep

Fawn, stag, doe,
each footfall so careful
in the fall meadow—
you show me how.

[1] Robin Wall Kimmerer relates the story, ANCIENT GREEN—*Moss, Climate, and Deep Time* in Emergence Magazine:

https://emergencemagazine.org/essay/ancient-green/

She also reads this story as a podcast at the same link. Robin Wall Kimmerer wrote, *Gathering Moss: A Natural and Cultural History of Mosses* in 2003.

A Fraction of Love

Shared Dreams

I relish her resonant *Yes,*
  growing *Nos,* garden-
    roughened hands,
   devotion to three cats,
that phoebe at the pool's edge,

her rescue of newts,
  bees, dragonflies, close
    attention to subtle textures
  and hues, her gifts
for human connection.

I roll toward my love—
  that radiant body so generous.
   I hold her dear and near, feel
  those strong arms, and rest
in the comfort of our aura.

These moments I treasure—
  yet don't we all fall
   asleep alone? I sink
  into my Beloved—
fountain of our dreams.

I touch my childhood scents

a sage leaf to roll and stuff
     into an acorn we'd hollow
          by scooping out its soft flesh.

Close to its base, we'd pierce
     a hole for a stem and
          make a smoker's pipe.

A wind-snapped pine branch—
     I hold that sappy split near
          my nose, and I'm back in the hills

of Haifa, the uncharted territory
     of my childhood, sailing pine bark
          in puddles. And the little old man

with missing teeth carrying
     a framework of sticks on his back
          bearing bagel rings, pretzels,

sunflower seeds in cellophane,
     whom we'd see
          on rare trips to town.

I am that acorn now. And the sage
    and pine? I'm still drenched
        in their scents.

And the long-gone bagel man?
    Perhaps from Poland to Russia?
        Perhaps, a concentration camp?

Who makes the time to ask
    as we buy their goods
        and hurry away?

Estero Outing

A light orange nose leads spindly legs toward a pool.
Her tongue laps the water. That tan coat—so close
to a wolf's—edges around the marsh grasses and
the brush that bears her name. Two pairs of ravens
settle on a hillock. Dark wings circle
against the skyline while ravens talk
in baritone croaks.

My daughter and I enter a pine grove.
She spots an olive-sided flycatcher,
hears pygmy nuthatches peeping, a grosbeak
and lazuli bunting's warbles. In the next patch of trees,
woodpecker drums and piercing calls—we catch sight
of one hairy and a northern flicker—
before opening onto the estero.

She spies an osprey, and I guess, from the flapping
white wings, another one. But my daughter directs me
to the large beak—a white pelican's enormous spread.
Harsh cries of Caspian terns rend the distance.
A red-tailed hawk swings by with a gopher in its claws.
Returning to the bridge, we see a mix of willets and
dowitchers on one side, and three gulls on the other.
A gull catches a crab, brings it to shore, pokes it
a couple of times and fiercely fends off the other two.

It swallows the crab whole and keeps it in its crop.
Crabs scuttle on the rocks underwater.
More and more become visible,
a few chewing and fighting over seaweed.
Last night, she cooked her first live crab.

And what if the Earth were as dear as my daughter?
I would turn to her to ask for help.
Can I fly to my friend's christening
or my niece's bat mitzvah?
Can I drive to Montana for a festival?
What would make you happy?

What will I give up for your sake, my dearest?

Each Wave

For Aunt Lisa (1922–2017)

Each wave crests with the color of deep, rich ore.
The ocean soothes my sadness
at what I learned from my cousin's call—
my aunt never told me she was one of the Kindertransport
children who crossed the Channel
after Kristallnacht in '38.

My mourning's silhouetted
by a black cormorant with outstretched wings.
The sun plays on the dark blue surface spattered
with grebes, loons, surf scoters. Palm weed lies scattered
on the shore like uprooted miniature trees.

The cries of two oystercatchers skimming low.
The child in me skips smooth stones.
A long fluid line of pelicans' notes
sails through the air.

In the Dream

i'm screaming at my brother,
get back you moron
you have 10 seconds
to step back—
do you understand?

my brother is hungry
he wants to eat
the food I'm cooking—
beans, rice, and corn

finally he yields

i'm too angry to share
too upset to chew

now my raw emotions
jolt and jangle the world

Roots

Sunlight cascading over
    the turning Japanese maple—
a fervor of coppery golds
    that hooks me to the spot.

I meet people who emit
    such beauty that I stand agape,
forgetting my own buried roots,
    coiled, waiting for

warmth and light to shoot,
    flower, shine, and—
when winter's pursed lips
    call—shed all.

Our Streams

The voices of my parents flow through
  and their parents', too, though less loudly,
and who can say what came with me
  from other lives? No matter our origins,

no matter our story, when we meet,
  our streams mingle. Showers might burst
to fertilize the plains, or instead, blindsided,
  back turned, the flow could plunge underground

waiting for that inner dowser to bring it 'round.
  Look in the mirror—my lukewarm disclosure
won't cut it. My half-hearted commitment
  to understanding you will never bridge

the yawning gulf. Our streams ache
  to make the music of waterfalls.

On a Cliff

Yellow flowering on tall, succulent
  red stems, seaside sunflowers,
    white yarrow, cow parsley bloom.

All cling to thin cliff soil—
  sink down roots, make their home.
    I hold fast to you, too.

Rain Devas

My heart's humming with the rain,
    fears of drought now drowned
        by these melodious steel drum sounds
           on skylight, roof, and deck.

Mist hangs in the trees,
    a sigh pours out into the land,
        joining puddles and rivulets—
          this unexpected boon of life.

Praise be for answered prayers,
    for each drop rolling down
        the oak's bare branches.

The View

Lemons, yellow shining lemons everywhere!
    Sloping hills, cloud, blue dome,
resonant greens bathe and balm.

Small bright orange sparks
    announce ripening satsumas.
A large red-tailed hawk atop a redwood

in the middle distance. Rustle of fresh oak
    and curved eucalyptus leaves
from the westward wind breaking the crest.

Perched on a trestle bench
    the owners left, I reap
the benefits of generosity,

sipping ginger tea from a thermos.
    These moments of solace
in a sea of man-made storms.

Rocks Overlooking Tomales Bay

And these massive boulders,
like stupendous crystals growing together
    for millions of years, stand sentinel
above the entry to Tomales Bay, ever watching
    the weathers and the seasons.

Some have large hollows, one graced
with a vault of intricate sandstone rings.
    Another boulder—
a giant's sagging face
    with mismatched eyes and drooping mouth.

Here the Miwok gathered to mash acorns
and make ceremony. Their grinding holes
    dot these rocks. I worship,
as they still do,
    this ancient congregation.

I circle these stones
before leaving for the shore,
    without realizing they'll be in me
forever.

New Moon's Old Tale

See the new moon rocking still
in the sky, high above darkening
pines and the streaming
cricket chorus. She speaks
of times before us
when her rhythms melded
waves, ice, and snow, and
she cradled life
in tidal pools as it waited
for just the right moment
to birth the very first
wrigglings.

And she speaks of time
after us when we will be
but a memory, a possibility
that flashed across, a little longer
than a lightning storm
yet shorter than all the ages
she has witnessed. And
there is no trace
of regret in her voice
but a quiet ring
whose peaks exceed
our imaginations.

As the crickets grow
louder with constant
changing tones, the moon
begins to soften,
or perhaps it's me,
chastened by her wonder.

Resurgent

Scented white candelabras set
  against dark green leaves of vine uncurl

with the five-lobed fig, California goldfields
  carpet the meadow, surge of fresh pine,

old chimes jingle in a new breeze,
  ceanothus in full blue bloom, rustle

of light off silver eucalyptus crescents,
  shower of Scotch broom, maroon

oak leaves opening like petals, daffodils
  beside a trestle table, swell

of birdsong threading in and out
  of silence, deep moss-covered bark,

silken sheen—another season's layer—
  and all the yellow sour grass

rippling by a sea of golden-tongued
  calla lilies in a patch of sun, ready

to spiral and unfurl, white-rayed
   yellow stars dance amid a pale blue ocean—

the first forget-me-nots cluster in gullies
  where rainwater drowns grasses
    in waves of resurgence.

Atascadero Creek

As I reach the creek today
  a Western pond turtle, sunning itself
on a rock, sees me and dives deep
  into the pool for shelter. No such shyness
for the California towhee skipping
  under the birch by the bridge
where water streams over stones,
  its musical trickling playing with fern
shadows, grasses, blackberry in bloom,
  oak, redwood, and all the willows'
naked roots anchoring these banks
  between a breezy meadow and the road—
you are my pulsing artery.

Oak Sky

Green, green, green
  oak canopy of glowing green,
    leaves sprout from your trunk
     like tufts of hair,
      curly, thick, and overflowing—
     reaching deep within,
      deep within—
       green tender tendrils.

A Fraction of Love

Tough as a tree trunk yet soft as leaves of lamb's ear.
She won't shirk what's in front of her.
She's no smoother-over or pleaser,
but a shade-giver.
Her crazy twists and turns will drive you dazed
into her meadow. She might shower
you with flowers without excuse or pretense
or strip you like a wild onion
until there are no layers of defense.
She doesn't flinch or shrink from knotted discord
but undoes us all.
Just a fraction of love
gives life her sparkling dress.
Just a fraction of love can never be said.

Low Tide

Bright orange starfish,
masses of mussels
on a rock outcrop.

Deep green anemones,
like spongy socks
glued to a boulder's base.

Seaweed holdfasts
and sea-green strands
awash like hair.

Purple starfish crusted
with white blend
among dark brown leaves.

Every inch of these
ocean rocks alive
and breathing.

The Shoal

The pelicans have struck bonanza.
　Wheeling and diving, they look
　　to spear their prey, opening beaks
　　　underwater, swallowing gulpfuls
　　　of ocean and fish. Some paddle
　on the surface; others, turning on the wind,
swerve back for more.

Now they've found a new shoal.
　The air overflows with flapping wings,
　　sudden plummets. Cries and scents mingle
　　　along the ethers as more and more
　　　seagulls, common murres, and guillemots
　join to feast on schools of anchovies
and sardines migrating north.

Led by longing's ache, I dive
　into my depths. Beneath
　　the thought waves and dancing
　　　undercurrents of desires,
　　I too find a shoal,
　as rich a feast as theirs,
another bonanza.

Crickets

I'm drunk under a half-moon
   on crickets' music
the color of hibiscus wine.

Their banks of sound—
   sizzling like sparking wires—

cascade into my ears, squeeze
   into my skin, spiral 'round my cells.

This orchestra sweeps over my soul.

Their waves carry me
   back to galaxies known only
in distant dreams.

Red Apple

I wash an apple in the kitchen sink
over a bucket to catch each precious drop
in drought-laden California. On its red skin,
streaked yellow-green, small light spots
shine like stars. I lift this cosmos
to my nose and breathe in its scent.

A thin stream of water bubbles up
from the well. Water—one and a half
gallons each flush. Water—the car, the lawn.
Water imprinted with codes
that tell of life's very beginnings,
O, holy lakes of the Sierra!

I put the apple in a bag to take on a walk.
I bring another bag to pick up trash
from our Mother's face. I'm not obsessive,
just restoring the beauty that sits outside my door—
the loquat tree my friend calls a giant birdfeeder
is also a sweet canopy of light and dark greens pulsing

with apricot-colored lights. Live oaks, bay laurels, eucalyptus
offer their limbs to thrushes and bugs. All hues
of pink and purple burst from sweet peas.
Floppy-eared bleating goats graze a neighbor's yard,

while across the way a brown gelding and two mares
maintain a field. Last winter they wore coats on cold,
damp days. Once more they're covered—
to protect them against the heat
we busily create each day to seal our fate.

O, skyscraping, arrogant creature.

Searching for seeds of wisdom, seeds of hope, inside
that juicy orb I find a light, a lamp,
and the core of a story threading through thousands
of years—those who've endured without
extinguishing that apple or its tree.

Lovechild

You're the forest of our dark running waters,
the pungency and heat of this eternal moment—
    our limbs interwoven, thighs clasped, your breath
rocking our cells, pores streaming salty droplets,
    our sighs and cries fill with your chorus, whose echoes,
alive in touch of hands, fill our cleansed tumbling words,
    open misted eyes—the lovechild borne in our hearts.

Thistledown

Indoor eyes cast down
  on bills, accounts, housework,
    plans, and musts—
      don't let this world

                escape you.

Scooting clouds, nobbly buds,
  children's screams, gurgling laughter—
    minds on tasks,
      worries, doubts,
          so many moments elude.

Branches spreading wild—
  all around hunger
    for a simple touch,
      will all this

                flit by?

Thistle in its purple prickly youth
  bowed, brown age
    soft downy head
      scatters

           in one season.

Web

Under the redwood leaves
woven strands bounce the sun.
In its center,
shaped like a Chinese character,
a spider plays catch.

Ablaze

Ablaze

Tall grasses sway, already
  sun-steeped gold
    in early May.

I will not wait for fire,
  I will not wait for flocculent clouds
    to break their vaults.

I pray for my heart
  to be set ablaze,

embrace these fields, thirsting
  trees, and birds
    in one note.

Opening Tree

Lit by lanterns of thousands
of pink filaments capped
with pollen pearls swaying in the breeze
below the just-opening leaves and
a crow's croak, *Haw! Haw! Haw!*
Haw! Haw! Haw!
The box elder's golden
ochre lichen against fresh green
shoots, branches against the sky—
blue with a light wash
of cloud—I become the soft
curling-under-my-toes grass, the sound
of dark, flapping wings, and
the nesting sparrow chasing.

Every Which Way

Every day the golden-brown candle flames
  on the black oak shine—fewer
    than the day before—slowly more
  of their twisting branches and spiraling
twigs revealed, caught mid-dance.

Some oaks wear a wild-forest fringe
  of terrible hair hidden under spring's
    sweet canopy. But their monstrous
    shadows cannot compare
  to our own sharp-fingered, knife-laden
jealousy or flashing anger—except

when the fires crack, and they turn into
  a riot of heat and hurtling flames. Though
    mostly they hang every which way, the last
      candle lights gleaming in the naked tree—
    the moon traveling untrammeled through
  its snaking branches as they stretch, poised
for the spirit winds to whirl them into dance.

Rose Petals
For Deborah

There's a secret fuse
   that keeps our love
   burning, at times so quietly,
like the early-morning hours,

at times explosive
   like the noon Saharan sun.
   There's a secret strand
woven long ago.

Only the seasons'
   gathered petals remind
   us, remind us,
beckoning with their fragrance.

Even Late in Life

Oak and alder shadows flit across the trail, reminding me of you. Bees and small cabbage whites among the goldenrod and blackberries take me back to a moment when I beheld in you a tender teen, a young woman, the holy child, all in your soft elder body. A willow overflowing with mistletoe green rounds and the *che, che, che* of a spotted towhee hold this moment and carry me along the cool, dusty earth welcoming my feet.

Cold Morning

I
Thick layers of ice crystals adorn the rail.
The granules turn into a mountain range.
I'm in the Alps yelping for joy—
howling for the long-gone wolf—
my myriad worries melt into the woods.

II
Water vapor steams off the redwood fence
to the midday sun's song, evaporating
the cauldron of my clotted cares.

Hawk on High

Almost translucent
  those white and black tail
and wing stripes backlit
  by the sun,
that ruddy redwood breast—
  circling on high,
calling, calling,
  I am king, I am king,
and the silence
          unchallenged.

Becoming

Redder than the lily's berry,
   smaller than forget-me-not, older
      than that mossy boulder across the path,
subtler than a fleeting sunset ribbon,
   taller than those redwoods, larger
      than the country I call home,
ease into the boundless—
   become those ever-flowing waters
      that some ache to drink and ford.

Raven's Eye
After "Ah, Ah," by Joy Harjo

Arak, arak   acorns patter down into meadow grasses,
tumbling silently to a stop.

Arak, arak   chattering high in the pines—no scrub jays,
but squirrels.

Arak, arak   hangs the mist dreaming on the ridge.

Arak, arak   spin wailing sirens six thousand miles away.

Arak, arak   fallen apples roll and spread. Their harvest
ties me here to the tree.

Arak, arak   a stag and three does saunter over, softly
sniff the air and bend their necks to earth.

Arak, arak   my younger brother's taken to the
Emergency Room. He is dying before me.

Arak, arak   an infusion of deep dusky pink streaking
through the clouds unites us.

Arak, arak   I dive into blackness to share this stillness
with you.

Angels Unaware

A spray of sparrows whirs
  out of coyote brush,
young laughter and
  yells spin around
red-berried cotoneaster.
  Blackberry leaves hedge
the road and power poles,
  a young redwood—its bark
so orange bright—
  stands sentry.

A motor revs, whines, and dies
  like the sun paling
through the dappled cloud.
  I'm dancing
with a hazel tree,
  a gold-leafed oak and bay,
all swaying on a hill.
  Birdsong, a dog's yip—
something or someone
  is listening in

Anemones

Soft turquoise-green edges,
   like rings or curls, wait
for the currents to bring them
    prey.

Purple-brown stems with large,
   rubbery leaves sway in the water
and in the air once the waves
    retreat.

I am one of so many,
   each on their own life
     intent.

On my way down Pinnacle Gulch

pale yellow buds, tightly bound
   cupules, open among green leaflets
   and the crash of rolling waves.

This bush thrives with coppery-red
   leaves of three, a coiling vine,
    some split dried pods, and a quiet
    chirping tucked into the hillside.

The Combination

Imagine you hold the key to this universe,
  the stars and blazing constellations.

Seasons unfold in their myriad ways,
  each one a silent click in a chain of ciphers—
  deep within you, the combination.

All depends on your loving witness—
  without it, skipped beats, jangling chords,
  a blaring horn mistaken for life.

You are the key to this universe.
  Now how will you be?

Smoldering

It's 11 a.m. and I'm writing in darkness.
  What light there is seeps yellow
    through banks of smoke-laden cloud.
  Raging fires in tinder-dry forests,
and my own fires rage, too.

Long-accumulated brush and debris
  I haven't cleared or tended
    or allowed my beasts to graze and roam.
  And where does my outrage go?
Will it douse or fuel the flames?

Light Vessels Take to Water

I'm ravaged by
   the sunset boats burning
      beside each other—
   moored next to cerulean
and soft-edged pink.

As this light sails
   in me, then it must
in you.

Pines and redwoods blacken
   the sky. The fiery vessels flame,
      pink melts
      while cars below race where?
   A bird begins to chirp. Who
will be home first?

A crescendo
   of reds. The boats
      slowly slide down the ramp
   of the hill
into the sea.

Calla Lily

Each day the cup grows larger,
   its lip curls farther, a miracle
      resting on its tall stem and

broad leaves, its delicate stamen
   a yellow glow through
      the translucent skin.

Although its core is not fully visible,
   we know its color and scent—
      its story, our story, the same.

New Home

The Master Gardener and his love
   have moved into my home.
      I no longer recognize it.

My small rooms give way
   to wild iris, cluster lilies,
      blue-eyed grass. Yellow

monkeyflowers and
   owl's clover abound
      in the living room. Walls

crumble, goats roam
   the hillside. By night,
      coyotes howl and romp.

What am I to do, now
   that my prayer's come true?

Leap

Every day I choose you
  and pray that in the moments
or hours of forgetting,
  you will choose me.

This river-driven,
  fire-cauldron body—
this mind, its constant
  crosswinds, rare gifts
of stillness when a candle
  shimmers—is yours.

Heart chambers carved
  by cataracts of blood—
all my wounds' aches—
  these were always yours.

I choose you because
  your fire leaps through all
my tangled undergrowth—
  nothing hides me from you.

First Storm

Skylights pulse
with drumming downpour—
the eucalyptus sways, loops,
and bends like a crazy fairground ride.
Rain sloshes on the decks, streams
down windows. Sheets slide
over gutters. The power goes out.

The last of the well water fills
a large cooking pot and buckets for the toilet.
Candles lit, flashlights ready, I turn
to a different power source—the one
that carpeted the deck with serrated beech leaves,
the one that released this Big Dipper, the one
that has me tied to each waking moment
and in the night deluges me in dreams,
the one without name whom I call on,
who responds in unexpected ways,
the one I've learned to trust beyond
silver, gold, and even blood,
beyond the carousel of good and bad.

Every Day You Call My Name

I remember Mom hollering my name throughout
  the neighborhood when I was seven. It must have
    penetrated into every home, bush, and tree.
      I wouldn't budge—mesmerized by my very
  first film, Abbot and Costello in the bullring,
on a reel-to-reel at the local grocer's.

How much of my life do I spend glued
  to a screen, ignorant that the principal
    actor in this drama isn't me? Now, when
      you call my name, sometimes in a whisper,
    sometimes a roll of thunder, I come running—
well, more a slowing, a-slow-ing into stillness.

Old Cat

Sitting on the deck, feet
     outstretched under a table,
I feel fur rubbing
     against my toes, hear a low purr.

It's become a ritual. She'll pause,
     slip her head through the railing,
or lie under my chair and then return,
     bend her ears, cheeks, whiskers
in this tug-of-love.

For years I gave her the least
     attention I could get away with.
She's older than I'll ever
     be, plays hungry, *riaows,*
just to bring out my love.

I've stopped caring how much
     or how little, bend mostly
to her will. Never understood
     her utter dependency
until my own illness and surgery.

Now, I'm the old cat.

Vessel

She pours creamy yogurt
  into the black bowl.
Pale moon peach slices
  slide off her spoon.
She tears plum pieces
  that run juicy yellow
and picks a few blackberries,
  just those ready
for release,
  that now gleam in her hands.

Honeysuckle scent surrounds
  her. The mockingbird and
acorn woodpecker calls—
  her morning music.
Hummingbird and pineapple sage,
  dandelions, and Oregon grapes—
the canvas. She mixes
  the fruit in her bowl
like a palette, scooping
  them into her mouth.

Streaks of white dance
  on the black ceramic
like coded calligraphy—

a message inscribed
to her love that she feels
   in her core—
yet knows that only
   in her vessel's depths
is the imprint
   fully planted.

Our Neighbor's Border

Acorn woodpeckers gather in
  early morning on the bare-limbed oak,
screeching *Jacobo, Jacobo, Jacobo…*

But first comes the sparrow hopping
  through the grasses, Queen Anne's lace
hanging in the air as I step toward
  the sloping bushes to pluck blackberries

into a bowl of stillness and stealth,
  while below, a doe with her young
dips and crosses our neighbor's border—
  no questions asked.

Temple Steps

As I puff and strain uphill
  past cow parsnip, poison oak,
    lupine, mallow pinks, vetch purples,
    coyote mint, all the colors of spring
      remind that I'm on temple steps,
      Her very own dance floor—
  each tree my sister/brother,
each rock my elder, every flower
a sparkling sequin of delight.

Sea Rise

They heave and glide
　　over rocks out at sea—
rush toward the shore
　　with a crash and a boom
closer, closer,
　　cascading, leaping,
they break.

I see the spray of white manes,
　　hear their thundering hooves
of furious foam
　　overrun the sands
until there is no strand.

Tethered

Inspired by John Donne, 17th c. mystic and poet

Oh, my Love,
  let me be tied to Thee
    as I am to the pump that feeds
    my blood and every cell
   with potent liquid
  all the while it sounds
in constant beat.

Coast Miwok Lands

Along the sands of Dillon Beach, that entry to Tomales Bay, wild frothing waves surge among hundreds of cormorants, diving pelicans, and seagulls fishing in these rich waters, their beaks finding treasure gleaming just beneath.

So many aviators set against the foggy hills across the bay. My son-in-law spots great antlered elk, too far for me to see. These choppy currents at the mouth too strong for them, or anyone, to swim across.

The wind and fog chill our fingers and toes. We sink our hands deep into our pockets and, braced and hooded, head into that fierce energy.

Ode to Ocean Fog

We have no mouth—we are all openings,
each pore welcoming molecules
of delicious moisture that trickle through
our capillaries, down our stems and trunks.
We are grass, weed, meadow flower,
coyote brush, apple, blackberry, and vine.
We sing and bow to the ocean fog
as she dances whirling through our leaves
and branches, swirling in with the cool evening,
stealing across the land over the pine
and redwood peaks into the oak and bay
tree valleys, now almost thick as wool,
suckling all life.

Intimacy

It's in the 80's. Midday. No shadow.
   I walk close to white
through purple hues of wild radish,
   reddish dock seed, newly planted oaks,
Sonoma wild grasses.

The call of a red-winged blackbird
   slows me. Make no mistake,
my mind had forsaken this vibrant scene
   for wishful thinking and unfulfillable desire,
when the intimacy I'm wanting is here.

Roiling Bay

Roiling waves joggle
  the red rocks jutting
    into the ocean, splashed
      with sea palm, ice plant
        and legions of mussels.

Listen—the whole bay
  sways from side to side,
    sizzling like boiling
      liquid. Surfers seeking
        the powers of Pacific waters

avoid this riptide beach—
  oh, creator, immerser, oh, wonder!

Rapt

The clocks have just gone
  back. Dusk has gathered
in its wings when a raptor
  silently lands on the line,

turns its large head with such ease
  this way and that. What, an owl?
I see its silhouette—
  those tufted ears the giveaway.

It takes off with a great stretch,
  vanishing into the gloom. Beating
through the mist in the light
  of a fingernail moon, joy rises.

The Heaven I Carry

This Finely Woven Tapestry

The serpentine meadow has woken
   from winter slumber
into a technicolor dream
   of cream cups, purple-petaled cluster-lilies,
golden poppies, and blue-eyed Mary.

A flash of white stripe slithers
   in her grasses. Bluebellies scuttle
under rocks. Great coppers, umber skippers,
   anise swallowtails, and bees have found
their haven. Let me, too, awaken
   into such full-bodied vision.

During the Drought

I take a pail of dishwater
  for the parched garden and pause.
Narcissus shoots rise, succulent cups
  of all sizes edged by delicious pink—
unfolding mandalas. Fine silvery-white
  hairs and creases on lamb's ears
stand out like copper-plate engravings.

I hear the whir of hummingbirds.
  Wherever I turn—birdsong.
This is heaven and I carry it.
  At this split second
the steel-blue clouds open—
  large pearly drops splash down.

Autumn

When autumn came along, I used to feel a certain sadness. Perhaps because I'm a child of summer, Earth's forces of slow withdrawal were painful.

Now each day I pick some fruits from the garden: beans, tomatoes, cucumbers, zucchini. Such abundance. More apples than I can handle—I put out a box "for free."

And the pink lilies that so dazzled and chained me with their scent—pregnant with seed. The African lilies, too. One last sunset-petaled flower remains on the dahlia bush. All the other heads and bodies have imploded, bearing their secrets.

Tiny, pale yellow flowers shaped like birds each hold a seed in their wings. Let me fly, too, with my cargo, to find fertile ground.

I welcome the darkening days as I've loved the long, springing evenings.

What appears to be dead, like the bare buckeye in early October, lives—the shiny nut's outer skin loosely wrapping all four seasons.

A bright orange-winged tarantula wasp and a tarantula spider grapple by the roadside. The wasp flips the spider over and injects its poison, then drags this huge spider, legs still kicking, before setting off to find a home for its prey. Life and death—nourishing each other.

With less drama, the oaks shed their acorns—elaborate sculpted cups of emptiness, their fruit already freed to feed the animals and us without distinction. Ah, autumn, come at your own pace. I am bound gladly by your rhythms.

Homegrown

I'm giving up joining the seminar of spiritual seekers,
    the zoom of fresh healers,
        to peel a garden onion—

planted by younger hands, keener eyes,
    with real enthusiasm for the chard, beans, basil,
        and all the herbs and vegetables filling their three beds.

My given task to take off those outer skins
    and revel in the fog flooding the hills, the bowing trees,
        as I dice a white potato,

slice bright orange carrots, green sugar snaps,
    yellow squash to add to the mix
        and listen to the music of the simmering pot.

Yes, a good hour has passed, and I feel filled,
    satisfied before the meal,
        by pounding summer savory

with mortar and pestle, sounds of sprinkled salt
    and pepper grinding, deep aroma and color of turmeric,
        the silences between the branches.

In Slowness

There's poetry in slowness,
    when you have no words,
the way a child looks with open eyes—
    all things arrive and stir inside.

Poetry when you hear sparrows
    while pulling clothes off the line.
Your basket fills. Waving treetops
    under curling clouds catch your glance.

The poetry of sitting down for a meal—
    holding hands in simple thanks.
When you lean down to pull a clump
    of weeds that leads to other wonders—

that spider's web, azalea blossom,
    weathered wood, plants and flowers
you could have sworn
    you'd seen before, yet…

A Fly

One summer door ajar,
   you follow the scents
     into the shade of
       a house—trapped!

I hear your drone
   and a light thwack
     against the glass.

I see your large red eyes,
   your bottle-green body
     on the windowpane
       prying and seeking.

If only I could deftly
   catch you and free you!
     But you don't settle
       for long.

Would it be kinder
   to clap my hands
     and squash you
       if I could?

In a short time
    you will lie still
        on the wooden sill,
        dry and ready
            for composting.

I travel briefly, too,
    in this house of glass.

June Long Light

June long light shines
   through clouds and pine tops
as quail come to the feeder for their evening seed.
Crests waggle while they do that wavy walk.
   It turns into a still standing
as if listening to silence.

I join them.
   We pass in and out of time.
They pick up their pecking.
Blackberry flowers toggle in the breeze.
   The light sinks. So many
colored coats—ah!

A motorcycle revving on the highway
   startles. A male quail struts closer.
The other three follow, poking and probing
cracks between the patio rocks.
   Then, with a whirr, they lift off as one.
Echoes of birdsong lighten the dusk.

On Awakening

I run the tap at a trickle,
  cup my hands, feel
    cold water coming
      from deep underground.

It chills my palms,
  shocks me awake
    when I splash my face
      and neck. I close

my one good eye,
  stare into darkness.
    Twice more, slowly, slowly,
      cupped hands are filled.

Is this a poem or
  a prayer? I rub my eyes
    and clean out
      the overnight. Help

my mind stay blank
  a little longer,
    so as not to blind
      this just-beginning light.

Dancers

Olive-green willows, filled with singing
   red-winged blackbirds, fence the wind—
      oh, it's good to be alive again.

Swallows swing overhead, dive swiftly
   across fields. The smell of hemlock seeds the air.
      Two figures, dead oak's offspring, bleached
         and sculpted by the dance of elements, twist.

Young oaks bear this year's shining
   apple galls, inviting like dappled fruit.
      Gusts blow, clouds scoot, bird calls travel—
      it's so good to be alive again.

Ragle Park
Southern Pomo Lands, Graton Rancheria

When I'm with the oaks
   leaning against their moss-covered limbs
as acorn woodpeckers whiz
   and weave loudly in the canopies

and cries of young children
   playing and whining—strung
to their moms—enter waves
   of green stillness springing from meadows—

a robin hops, listening to others' calls
   and the spotted towhee scratches
among the lost years' leaves,
   a yellow swallowtail swoops along

the sun's rays—then
   for a little while, I'm freed.

"Return again, return again . . ."
   Title from a song of the Jewish New Year
   embodying Tshuvah, or returning to oneself

My soul is a field
that life tills and tends.
Perhaps rocks need to be broken,
or dips and holes need to be filled.
Perhaps sand, or seaweed, or humus added
before it can yield something
lovely like a potato, maize, or a sunflower.

And, like a field, my soul longs to be sung to
while I water, compost, cover-crop, and putter.
For what am I born for if not to praise?

And the Earth will praise us, too,
even as she takes our bodies
back into her arms.
We are so intimate,
why act as strangers?
Like an open hand,
our secrets are all known.

During how much of each day can I drop
my false faces to be naked before you ?

I count on you to raise me up
when, like a child learning to walk,
I fall again and again and again.

Now, I sing to you,
Be alive in me—
a little more, a little more.

In the Mouth of the Wind

I'm stopped by a cliff and a broken
    pencil. I sharpen it on sandstone.
      Cliffside grasses and lupines wave

while rocks make spray leap like mustangs.
    Sand streams low. High white cloud, sun.
      Pounding *whoosh* of air and water.

A turkey vulture wobbles in the wind,
    its black and white underside hovers
      like a kite. Surf crashes.

Two black oystercatchers and a perched gull
    eye the mussels. Five moon-curved
      dunlin beaks pick and jab at the water's rim.

Blasts and gusts keep pushing me aside
    to be a pencil in the wind's mouth.

Too Simple

Listen to the water
   tumble in the weir. Bending
      low, it sounds louder, clearer.

Across the stream
   a winged reflection flits.

The creek's music
   fills to the brim
      beside the highway.

I peer up at bay,
   redwood, willow, birch,
      a lone apple tree.

Is happiness this simple?
   When did you first lurch
      into my heart?

Ocean

Your surging roar answered by sea lions
  on the granite isle—that sumptuous white froth
    swirling over rocks, fertile waves
    of kelp, greens, jellyfish, and shells
  flung each tide on the shore,
gulls arcing and surfing with the wind,
brown pelicans in vee lines
  effortlessly skimming your face,
    cormorants bobbing or gathered on jutting rocks,
    the red dragon kite floating above—
  birth of beginnings—
carry me into your dreams.

Blossom Shower

Once more brimful, the privet billows in high
   summer breeze, its creamy flowers tilt to
buzzing wings and ants locked in steadfast silence—
   each floret a yellow cup for all to drink.

Filigree shadows begin to lengthen,
   the smell of berries as autumn beckons.
Thousands of tiny blooms rain down
   on the warm paving, packing the gaps.

Softly pour those scented blossoms
   in the night to fill the cracks and fissures
in my heart. Don't let me notice your
   healing kiss, so, like the vulture's flight,
it may bless the land and merge with
   the uplift woven by the turning seasons.

We, the Healers

Her Unbroken Giving

I
It will happen unplanned,
like the gopher burrow
that diverts the waters
rushing down the hillside
from their appointed channels
to a flat patch—
where pools now gather, sit,
trickle through layers of
silt, sandstone, and clay
to the aquifer
that feeds the well.

II
When I was a child
and someone hurt me
my petals closed,
my shell snapped shut,
I burrowed underground.

And what do I believe
will coax this wounded Earth
to show me Her face
in all weathers?

Crossing the Ocean
Intensive Care Unit

Malena, the night is rocky
  the night is long
    you hold me here
      in your care

as waves toss my body.
  I hear your voice
    in this cold, cold sea
      filling me with warmth.

For twelve hours my vessel's
  buffeted by rolling
    swells; for twelve hours
      by my side you sail.

Malena, how can I thank you?
  Your shift is over—
    my journey's just beginning
      at day's break
  in this body newly built.

The America I Love

Three weeks in hospital in San Francisco, my three
lead surgeons: one American born; one from Iraq with
a Lancashire accent, soft as its misty rain; one from
India with the auspicious name, *Prasad*, "blessed food."
An aide sings a folksong to me in a language from
Northern China, her hand holding her apron as if she's
dancing in traditional costume. A tall African American
orderly, born and raised in the city, who works two jobs
to make the rent, wheels me into the operating room.
An accountant from Sierra Leone via Paris collects the
garbage on the wards, goes to night school, and hopes
to bring his wife and daughter here. A young male nurse
from a Filipino family tends to my dressing and teaches
me patience.

Dusty Lane

When the pink blossoms unfurl,
their five petals cupped around light
yellow stamens, soft leaves budding
from new growth, my heart can't
help but open
                              to the notes tumbling
through the air—mistletoe wedded
to a branch puts forth its spiraling green,
whiffs of heady scent rise from
wisteria gone wild in riotous glory
up and down every oak, bay, fir, and plum
lining the lane, each upright petal
shimmering like a fire—
then I have touched heaven, and all
I touch is now made whole.

Antidote to the News

petal upon petal
  pale purple
    hot coral
      saffron
        siren yellow

among serrated leaves
  and spiders' webs
    each five-rayed floret
     clusters into
       a shining globe

a simple patch
  to mend my heart

Forest Bathing

Who can match that delicacy
of palette, that ethereal touch—
pools of forget-me-nots
beside wooded paths?

First Day of Spring

and my feet, at last, in water
    with dunlins, godwits, willets.
        Waves break on outcrops—

        such soothing sounds.
    Children draw parents
to the ocean's edge, toes alive again

to pebbles, crab claws, shells.
    Seaweed hair covers the rocks.
        Trills from the cliff.

The waves, too, carry
    a conversation that fills
        the air and stirs

our elements. Golden
    plates of jellyfish await the tide.
        Some bear orange sacs, others

        maroon tails. A litter of mussels—
gulls' treasure. Heel, sole, ball,
into the soft, hot sand my toes curl.

Path to the Redwood Grove
With thanks to Terry Ehret

Light streams through the dark
  of distant trees,

plays on a patch of blackberry
  lit by the coo of a mourning dove.

Supple bay trunks overarch
  the shallow creek.

Below sorrel banks
  reflections trickle.

This soft needle path threads its way
  across a footbridge.

Past a water tank and chugging pump,
  a redwood world greets me.

My steps echo
  into stillness.

Twin trunks rise three hundred feet
  from a mother base.

Sword ferns, woodwardia, maidenhair
  everywhere.

In the sculpted grottos woodrats nest
  and small webs nestle in folds.

The double whistle of a hermit thrush
  laces the towering silence.

Blackened trunks—old fire
  or a lightning bolt?

I bow to these beings
  who survive it all.

Roots of Terror, Seeds of Peace

Boom! Go the guns. *Boom! Boom! Boom!*
Four years old, I stand on the balcony with my family
watching an Egyptian battleship in Haifa Bay,
overwhelmed by Israeli jets. "How stupid!" mock
the adults. "They thought they could shell us in broad
daylight." The captured ship on exhibit
for taunts and humiliation. It's 1956.

      •

Downtown, tanks roll by, sailors with white caps
and rifles slung across their shoulders proudly march.
Low-flying thunderous displays—
it's Independence Day—followed by
deafening fireworks terrify me.

      •

Arabic music floats from the radio—
my mother yells, "Turn it off, I can't stand it!"
So we miss the rhythms of the round *tar, doumbek,* and
flute—camels striding through the desert, their bells
ringing, carriers of food and hope.

      •

And the Druze girl who often falls asleep
on her desk, blond braid, care-worn face.
I, now seven, know nothing of her life,
or why she keeps missing school.
My father says, "The men wear baggy trousers
to catch the Prophet when he's reborn."

I'm following my three-year-old son
who's pedaling his red and green wooden trike,
feet flying along the path to reach the playground.
We're in a park in North London, early 1980s,
behind me, three Tibetan orange-and purple-robed
monks. The elder calls out, *"Indien?"* It flashes
through me—he may be seeing a past life. It's true
that at 22, I traveled overland through souks
and chai shops, all the way to India, but I answer, "No,
I was born in Israel." After a while, he ricochets,
"Ah, Arabe." I'm shocked. No one has ever called me an
Arab. Perhaps from his perspective,
there is no real difference!

> *Oh, Isaac and Ishmael, together you weep.*
> *Hagar and Sarah, your tears water this land.*
> Damned are they who say, "We want peace,"
> yet neglect to tend their inner tree.

Blessed are the peacemakers, Palestinian and Israeli.
Blessed be they in their daily tasks.
May their olive trees flourish

The Day She Passed

We sat around in our pajamas,
stunned. I'd waited some long hours to tell
our daughter once she woke. Dr. Andrew
drove round to certify the death and left.
We sat around waiting
for the morgue folks to fetch the body. Two men came.
They needed help. We wrapped her up in a sheet
and carried the stiff, cold corpse to the van.
Then we sat around some more
until an impulse entered—*Shall we go to the beach?*
The ocean lay just twenty minutes away. All that water
seemed a good place for tears. Our daughter
perked up, *Let's take my shovels and the big
ones, too.*

Down on the sands that salty wind blew.
Life continued as if it didn't know our dearest
wife and mother had gone. I wanted to shout out
the news. But the sun just shone
and a couple with a dog kept throwing a ball
into the waves. Our daughter said, *I want to be buried.
Dig a hole for me!*
She used the plastic shovels. We dug a pit three feet deep—
a vast emptiness—she climbed inside.
Cover me up!

I'll cover you only if you'll get yourself out, I said.
I loosely shoveled the still damp sand
until only her hands and hatted head
and braids showed through. I left a couple

of plastic tools and took the longest walk
to the ocean's edge, still within
earshot, but far enough away
to cry and pray.
Minutes trickled slowly beside the infinite shore.
After what struggles had our daughter freed herself?
Wordless, we both grasped
that, however long the road, somewhere
she knew the way.

California Wildfires
2017 and 2018

Red smoke sun,
 choking air—
  strange quiet
   hangs the light,
    coyote brush
     glows stark.

Small birds call—
 listen to a pulse—
  I breathe in fear
   through a mask—
    the future flickers.

I turn to
 the turning maple,
  the flowering loquat.
   They give and give
    until they cannot.

Sea Confetti

The seaweed lay like rose confetti scattered
  on the sands and the water gleamed
    all yellows of the sun. Waves purled and crested
    with a quiet swish, rushing out again
  like a netted wish. Black cormorants atop black rocks.

Inland, quite close, the fires scorched, the air
  thick with ash. Here, gulls and sanderlings
    at the water's rim ran, probed, and splashed.
    And in these diverse 'scapes I'm stung
to ease the heat on tomorrow's young.

The Whale's Song

You are the last gray—
the last ocean bottom farmer beyond
             lonely,
                      lost,
                             terrified.

You swim in waters too warm
for your ancestors and kin,
pickings so slim
                      you starve.

You have danced
in the depths for eons,
the ocean's moods and moons
embedded in your bones
and mottled skin.

You bear her barnacles
                      and
                             grief.

Your surging into the deep—
that constant churning
kept the planet's plankton
                      balance.

How will we live now,
our young, foolish species?

You are the last gray—

wailing.

Fall Wedding

Silver train,
dazzling origami cranes,
a thousand threaded
suspended by
royal blue beads—
the bride's tribute
to her mom,
long-passed.

Weeks ago,
side by side,
the groom and bride
built a stage.
Days before the feast
their friend baked
latticed fruit pies
and squashes
from a neighbor's
yard. Yesterday,
the groom scrubbed
the kitchen down
to prepare carnitas.

Across both sides
of the deck, tables

arrayed in an L,
each one bedecked
with a bouquet,
sea-smoothed pebbles,
electric candle lights.

My daughter—effulgent,
French braids,
silk brocade,
weighted floral train.
"Ah!" escapes lips
as she and I glide
through twenty-seven
years toward the stage.

I halt. Release.
She steps up, transfixed
by her lover's eyes,
pledges, "Every day
I choose you."
Asters shine,
zinnias bask,
dahlias burst.

We, the Healers

I want to be like that couple
at the top of the hill stealing a kiss
in the wind and rain.

Maybe you had a happy childhood.
Maybe you watched your parents dance
and didn't see them crush each other.
Maybe their words didn't lacerate,
and you inherited only your ancestors' wounds.
*The roast's delicious / not bad / a little dry / not as good
as last time.* My family didn't talk about what mattered most.
Did yours?

We're the walking wounded
who light a stranger's face
when we see
another wounded walking.

Is it foolish to want to rise
into clouds, weak to fall
like rain?

Worlds

Cedar waxwings perch in a row
  of pines. The sun highlights that yellow
spot on the tip of their tails,
  while lavender blooms

abuzz with bees from nearby hives.
  A fawn forgets itself, nibbles a plum
from my palm. A half-moon
  follows me in broad daylight.

What worlds enter when I sleep!
  On waking I'm surprised to be here.
Sipping tea in silence, all around me
  cells cry, *So much music! So much music!*

Tucson Shooting

I visit a new friend
in the rain-greened California hills.
His voice reverberates with aftershock:
     nineteen shot
  in Tucson, Arizona!

     He knew one of them.
Got his coffee from
the same store as his friend
     on that fateful morn.

     Our tears flow onto the saguaro.
Will not prickly winds
hammer and whip
     while Chip and Hannah
  carry guns everywhere?

     Like the swallowtail butterfly,
we cup our wings to freedom—
lift our faces
     to the sun.

     We bare arms
and bodies to its rays
pray to raise our children
     free from shadowing fear.

Rich veins of peace run through
our canyons, hills, mountains, and
parched earth. The saguaro thirsts
for blossoming rain.
Which way will we aim?

Arizona's state flower is the saguaro cactus blossom. Its state butterfly is the two-tailed swallowtail.

The shooting took place in 2011 during a constituent meeting held in a supermarket parking lot with Gabby Giffords, representing Arizona's Eighth Congressional District. Giffords was shot in the head at point blank range and miraculously survived. She and her husband, Mark Kelly, went on to become ardent advocates for gun control.

Peace Presence

The frost brings out
the whorls and swirls that flow
    like fingerprints
through these redwood deck planks.
      *

While Thich Nhat Hahn slowed
the whole anti-war march
    walking with mindful presence,
thousands of fraught, pained people
    came to their senses.
      *

When do I make time
to look at the shelf
    instead of the books?
To touch the grain
    and let the pine feel me?

Every Parent's Worst...

The Peshawar school massacre, in northern Pakistan,
took place in 2014

Peshawar, "City of Flowers,"
    I sing for you.

Their years have flown
   like rapid Himalayan-melt,
all one hundred and thirty-two
   children—their past, present,
and future loves and labors taken.

In daytime they came—
   like a hunting pack—
to the school they littered
   with carcasses.

I travelled through you in '74,
   a twenty-two-year youngling,
     what did I know of suffering?

Columbine, Cold Spring, Chardon,

Sandy Hook, Sparks, Marysville,

Townville, San Bernardino, Douglas,

Santa Fe, Red Lake, Nickel Mines,

Aztec, Marshall, Union City,

　　so near, so near,
unbearably chilling.

And we, over 200,000,000
　　strong parents and grandparents
when will we face our part?
　　When do we put our foot down?

Uvalde, I sing you a song,
　　a song of lament
　　　　to soothe my tears.

　　　　I wait in dread.

In the Land

There's a peace in the land,
    a peace in the land.
        Morning fog and cloud dome the sky.

Across the view fly a pair
    of Eurasian collared doves.

In Glastonbury or Machu Picchu
    Mecca or Uluru/Ayers Rock,

you'll find resonating in you
    a deep peace in the land.

Cars pace the highway, a scrub jay
    pecks ripening apples.

When you're in the temples
    of Kyoto or shrines of Srinagar
        or your own backyard,

each time you open
    there's peace in the land.

In Gratitude

Thank you, Terry Ehret, for your wonderful inputs as editor of this book and all my previous ones. Thank you, Nan Hopkin, for your insightful suggestions and for supporting my writing these past twenty years. And thank you, Carolyn Miller, for your copyediting and many ideas.

These poems would not exist without Earth's daily inspirations. Noticing Her tiniest ways raises my spirits and makes me want to bow low.

I am deeply grateful to my teachers, who blew on the embers of my heart and fanned the flames. I especially thank Llewellyn Vaughan-Lee, who, since the year 2000, has shared so generously his perceptions of Earth's needs and plight.

Thank you to Judyth Greenburgh for a gorgeous cover. And thank you, dear John Peterson, for believing enough in my work to birth our fourth book!

I'm also grateful for the journals and anthologies that published these poems:

Abrazos: DoveTales Tenth Anniversary Anthology: (DoveTales, 2021) "Her Unbroken Giving" and "Ablaze"

Birdland: "Antidote to the News," "The Combination," and "Her Unbroken Giving"

California Quarterly: "New Moon's Old Tale" and "New Home"

The Freedom of New Beginnings: Poems of Witness and Vision from Sonoma County, California (Ed. by Phyllis Meshulam, Poetry Crossing Press, 2022): "Ragle Park"

The Mindful Word: "Resurgent," "Roots," and "In Slowness"

Quiet Diamonds (Orchard Street Press, 2021): "Worlds"

Sufi Journal: "Dusty Lane" published as "The French Garden's Garden," and "First Storm."

About the Author

Born on a kibbutz, Raphael Block spent his boyhood playing on the hills of Haifa. His family returned to London as he turned nine, where learning British English shaped his ear for sound. In 1993 he moved to Northern California with his American wife, Deborah Simon Block, and their three-year-old daughter, Theadora. After Deborah passed away from cancer in 2002, it became Raphael's privilege to raise their child.

As a teacher, Raphael worked with children under five for many years in London's inner city. In California he taught all grade levels, including teaching Waldorf, and also worked with kids with disabilities. A Sufi meditation practice and two life-threatening illnesses, Crohn's and MDS, a form of leukemia, have played major roles in intensifying his appreciation and gratitude for the moments of each day.